Agates in the Sand
Thoughts of a Common Person

By Richard L. Narver

authorHOUSE®

AuthorHouse™
1663 Liberty Drive
Bloomington, IN 47403
www.authorhouse.com
Phone: 1-800-839-8640

© 2012 Richard L. Narver

No part of this book may be reproduced, stored in a retrieval system, or transmitted by any means without the written permission of the author.

Published by AuthorHouse 12/5/2012

ISBN: 978-1-4772-9269-3 (sc)
ISBN: 978-1-4772-9268-6 (hc)
ISBN: 978-1-4772-9267-9 (e)

Library of Congress Control Number: 2012921811

Any people depicted in stock imagery provided by Thinkstock are models, and such images are being used for illustrative purposes only.
Certain stock imagery © Thinkstock.

This book is printed on acid-free paper.

Because of the dynamic nature of the Internet, any web addresses or links contained in this book may have changed since publication and may no longer be valid. The views expressed in this work are solely those of the author and do not necessarily reflect the views of the publisher, and the publisher hereby disclaims any responsibility for them.

it was
a simple
poem about
how i
would always
love her
that made
her cry.

Richard L. Narver

i tiptoed
into bed
so as
not to
wake my
wife, but
before I
could get
to sleep -
she curled
a leg
around me
and winked.

she brought
me over
a six-pack
so I
let her
leave her
shoes under the bed
while I
thanked her.

———————

summer -
cold beer
and a
hot woman.

Richard L. Narver

(early years)
i dream
of finding
a blonde
who owns
a Corvette
and a
liquor store.

(later years)
my nightmare
is finding
a blonde
who owns
a Corvette
and a
liquor store.

the flies
(in my opinion)
have a
right to
buzz around
hot dogs
and potato
salad but
when they
land in
my beer
their wings
should be
removed.

Richard L. Narver

the poem
i didn't
write today
will be
profound
for those
who prefer
silence.

———————

simplicity
is not
that simple.

Agates in the Sand

a blank
page is
not a
bad thing.

Richard L. Narver

an
evening's work
fills my
wastebasket
with paper wads.

───────────

my life's work -
typed in
one hour
and read in
(approximately)
fifteen minutes.

───────────

tonite-
i tore
up everything
i wrote
except this.

the value
(generally)
of a belief
is not
whether it
is true
or false
but what
it does
for people.

---

my friend-
may you
go with
God but
wait until
He calls.

Richard L. Narver

Fall's light
(like life)
quickly turns
to darkness.

———————

sacred place-
in the
light above
the clouds.

———————

as the
sun rises
a cougar
screams.

———————

breakers crash below-
gull soars overhead.

memories from the grave

I

i traveled from oasis to oasis
in my youth, between campsites
i searched for unknown paths.
in my middle age, I overcame
the desert's illusions
and followed the caravans.
in my old age
i looked over my shoulder
and found I had left
no footprints of my own

II

a storm destroyed my marker
and covered my grave with waste.

Richard L. Narver

the candle
(unfortunately)
was blown
out by
an unexpected
breeze.

---

the cougar's
steps were
not heard
as it
stalked
the hunter.

---

day's end
journey's end
darkness begins.

---

wings flutter
dying screams.

the
trumpet man's
blues full
of despair
drifted into
the night.

---

short days
gray clouds
rustle of
dry leaves-
empty promises.

---

twilight
purple clouds
a light breeze
a brief time
(to reflect)
before darkness.

Richard L. Narver

no one
has seen
me come
no one
has seen
me go
i live
in the
weeds and
glow on
Sunday.

---

ignorance-
like blindness
prevents us
from seeing
what is.

before
conception and
after death
there is
darkness.
in between
there are
precious moments
of light.

Richard L. Narver

pitch with
your head
it is
(hopefully)
smarter than
your arm.

———————

yesterday's game-
don't waste
your time
on trying
to change
the score.

———————

(for Yogi)
the final
score
is hard
to beat.

oh, God -
i need
a great
thought.

---

i waited
(patiently)
for a
great thought
but fell
asleep
before
it arrived.

---

words
most wanted
never found.

Richard L. Narver

blank page
full of
wisdom.

the assistant editor
returned my
haiku with
a check list
that looked
like it
suffered from
smallpox
so I sent
it back
to him
in a
coffin.

Richard L. Narver

poet's eyes
see too
much pain.

———————

my writing
comes from
hard times.

generally-
sending a
work to
a publisher
is like
sending a
child to
war -
nothing good
will come
of it.

―――――――――

i don't care
what your
rules are,
i am sending
the whole thing.
If you
are the
"eleventh editor"-
may you live
a long
and good
life.

Richard L. Narver

silence
between friends
speaks.

without
a word
the heart
knows.

"friendship"
can change
like the
weather.

Richard L. Narver

after many
years of
pulling heavy
carts, the
ox fell
and suffered
a broken leg.
thereupon,
the owner
shot the ox
and fed it
to his dogs.

in dawn's
grey light
i walk
through the
silent fields
alone in
my thoughts.

---

pre dawn-
the mist
lies briefly
upon the
field, so
fresh and
sweet.

---

grey clouds
short days
rustle of
dry leaves.

Richard L. Narver

we waste
our lives
in small
matters.

———————

life -
a moment
to love.

when
i
looked into
her eyes,
i knew
i had
loved her
since the
beginning of
time.

―――――――――

her tears
(with love)
fell upon
my chest.

Richard L. Narver

the
piano man's
haunting
love songs
fill the
night and
stir the
heart.

---

the heart
(though blind)
is our
navigator.

---

love
(most likely)
only reason
for living.

my opinion-
nine out
of ten
editors should
be shot
and the
tenth one hanged.

---

sending
my work
to a
publisher
is like
looking for
a light
in the
abyss.

Richard L. Narver

there can
(unfortunately)
be more
Mondays than
days in
the week.

―――――――――

time
is full
of shit.

―――――――――

after lunch
the world
looked better
even though
it wasn't.

―――――――――

big money
like shit
stinks and
draws flies.

people
without vision
(poor souls)
see races
rather than
human beings.

───────────────

ignorance
like blindness-
prevents us
from seeing
what is.

───────────────

they lived
and died
in darkness-
never knowing
their darkness
was self
imposed.

Richard L. Narver

life-
so much
depends on
how you look
at It-
and what
you give
to it.

―――――――――

a
line in
the sand
(drawn deep)-
covered by
a breeze.

―――――――――

with darkness
there comes
the horror
of a
wasted day.

Papa's story-
frozen leopard
so close
to the
western summit
(the House
of God),
so close…

Richard L. Narver

the sheep
in the fog
invisible
(except to the shepherd).

───────────────

day ends
(suddenly)
without warning.

───────────────

pond-
fish jump-
ripples.

───────────────

the lamb
(in panic)
ran until
it died.

baseball season
(like life)
begins with
the hope
of a
new day.

Richard L. Narver

    very late
comes too fast.

---

    even
   a dog
if cornered
 will fight
  Pavlov

---

  old age
(generally)
humiliates us.

---

 the clock-
always ticking.

---

times edge-
(too close)
step carefully.

we can
have vision
but not
be able
to see
what is.

―――――――

cruelty
(not death)
is our
greatest
problem.

Richard L. Narver

life-
a poker game
hide some aces.

———————

life
(generally)
short path
to nowhere.

———————

life's road
a cul de sac.

———————

life-
a series
of ongoing
adaptations.

Agates in the Sand

early evening
the purple
sky and
the cool
delta breeze.

---

light breeze
through the
pines softly
sings a
love song.

---

as i warm my hands
by the fire,
a wolf's cry
breaks the silence.

Richard L. Narver

at sunset-
an old
man fishing
in a
slough with
his dog
asleep at
his feet.

---

before the
day ends
leave the
plow in
the field
and climb
the mountain.

in darkness-
a candle's
dying glow.

---

pre dawn-
the mist
briefly lies
upon the
fields so
fresh and
sweet.

---

delta breeze
(old friend)
savior of
my evening.

Richard L. Narver

home
from work-
smell of
pot roast-
hallelujah!

———————

she
smiled, undressed
and began
drinking my
wine.

her eyes
(always)
said they
loved me.

Richard L. Narver

lover's test-
light of day.

---

in
the night
she lay
upon my
chest and
we became
one -
forever.

---

her love
(most needed)-
gift to
start the
new year.

without love
there is-
nothing.

───────────

the heart
never forgets.

Richard L. Narver

she talked
the most
when she
had nothing
to say.

---

anxiety-
(after a
few beers)
long line
to the
rest room.

---

true love:
kissing a spouse
who has a
runny nose.

she was worried
that she might
have appendicitis
so she
shaved her
legs.

Richard L. Narver

love-
like light-
eternal.

first love
(though absurd)
always hurts.

---

love
(always)
ends too soon.

---

sex
without love
destroys the
heart.

---

love-
slowly lost
in cold nights.

---

love-
is our
miracle.

Richard L. Narver

      time-
     its pace
   is frightening
       as it
   races around
    the track.

———————

dead friends
(so many)
  live in
 my heart.

———————

the graveyard-
silent except
  for the
digger's cursing.

the old
get lost
in the
shuffle-
but the
dance
goes on.

Richard L. Narver

he died
before he
made it
to the summit-
like most
of us.

the play
(a comedy)
ends when
all the
clowns die.

―――――――

from
the summit
the view
is clear-
what appears
small-
is.

―――――――

the truth
is close
but oddly
is seldom
seen.

Richard L. Narver

years pass
dreams die.

———————

time
(our child)
travels beyond
our existence
to measure
endless sequence.

———————

the old man
(bent over)
took small
steps against
the wind.

———————

candle flickers
darkness near.

———————

clock ticks
candle burns.

a lie-
the truth about
its author.

Richard L. Narver

truth-
(generally)
beyond our
vision-
but present.

---

see people
(though painful)
as they are.

---

reality-
indifferent
as stone.

it is good to not
know what is true
when it is false.

---

appearance
(generally)
is deceptive-
look into
the heart.

---

deceit-
office cornerstone.

---

see through
the mask-
see the
hidden face.

Richard L. Narver

    betrayal
  like smiling-
  easily done.

mountain
too steep-
yet i
climb.

Martin's dream
lost in
harsh light
of day.

---

prejudice-
see it clearly
even against
prejudiced people.

Richard L. Narver

    learn from
    the past
    but don't
    carry it
    with you.

---

    belief
    (most likely)
    a blanket
    for a
    long night.

---

    i am
    (God knows)
    a leper
    seeking the truth.

---

    caravans
    stumble along
    old paths -to nowhere.

i reached
for the
rose but
only got
pricked by
the thorns.

Richard L. Narver

for a
moment i
was uncertain
as to
whether i
should propose
but after
she stepped
into the
shower - i
grabbed my
coat and
ran.

night woman
my fire
in the
cold.

---

in
the night
i was
"freezing" -
so i
gave her
twenty bucks
to save
my life.

Richard L. Narver

a good tip
keeps their
mouth shut.

―――――――

my dog
left his
fresh shit
on my
front porch
to show
(no doubt)
how much
he enjoyed
his meal.

being alone
(at night)
will kill
the heart.

---

we never
fool
our heart-
we torture it.

---

love's absence-easy to see.

---

winter's night
no hope-
freezing.

---

loneliness
no-one
to hold.

Richard L. Narver

the heart
(though blind)
is our
navigator.

for Craig
(in memory-)
we have
many difficulties
in life
but the
death of
a young
person is
at the
top of
the list.

Richard L. Narver

death-
(always)
so close.

---

moment
before death-
the mind's
last scream.

---

the boy
started laughing
during the
funeral and
couldn't stop.

---

death
(generally)
comes too late
or too soon-
blind idiot.

old graveyards
full of
young dreams.

---

each moment
too vital
to waste.

---

time
(always)
our road
to oblivion.

---

our play
(our life)
hysterical.

Richard L. Narver

death-
too busy
to help
the suffering.

––––––––––––––

death- candle without a flame.

time passes
(we pass)
everything passes.

God's
children cry
too long
at funerals.

---

he died
(slowly)-
without hope.

---

the dead-
horribly dead.

---

death
(without illusion)
eternal nothingness.

Richard L. Narver

time
(without pause)
travels beyond
our existence.

———————

time
(too often)
lost in
day's work.

———————

last moments
(too soon)
dreams lost
forever.

———————

life-
lost struggle
against
nothingness

first love
(forever)-
haunts us.

---

love - heart's gift.

---

lost love-
hurts
forever.

---

our life-
endless search
for love.

Richard L. Narver

"love"
(generally)-
lost at
sunrise.

———————

life
(wasted)-
without love.

———————

the heart
in pain
cries for
a lover.

———————

loneliness - more fatal than cancer.

it is
not enough
to see,
you have
to act
in accordance
with what
you see.

───────────────

see
(everything)-
as it is.

Richard L. Narver

when I
was a child,
i shot
a lion
in my
grandmother's
back yard.
i showed
her the lion-
(bless her)
she saw it.

───────────

understand
a person's
needs and
you will
understand
them.

(to Clint and Heather)

life's most
precious moment
is the union
of two hearts.

two hearts
become one
as they prepare
to travel
through deep canyons,
over mountain peaks,
and beyond horizons.
two hearts
seeking love
beyond time.
…
may your love-
be eternal.

Richard L. Narver

(to Nicole and David)
love comes
from the dawn
of human life
it is
our calling
for the hearts
to become one.
two hearts
as one
travel through
unknown dimensions
of time -
be assured
love's goodness
will never die.
may your love
be strong
may your love
be eternal. - bless you

purpose
(our strength)-
to create
a better life.

Richard L. Narver

want nothing-
it will
help you
serve
others.

---

crying
in sad times
is strength-
its absence
is weakness.

---

live
(for goodness)-
make your mark.

intimacy
(sacred)
never lose it.

---

old friends-
(precious)-
best friends.

---

friend
(somehow)-
lost without
a word.

Richard L. Narver

vision
is to
see in
darkness.

blind shepherd
(in faith)
searches for
lost sheep.

Richard L. Narver

my friend
i hope
you find
what is.

———————

may good purpose
(like a blessing)
always guide you.

———————

my friend-
climb the
summit
and
make it
your home.

purpose
never dies.

---

life
(only)-
is.

---

my children
are the
meaning of
my life.

---

truth about
our life-
too close
to see.

Richard L. Narver

the dead
only live
in us.

───────────

life
(most likely)
has no
meaning
except what
we give
to it.

───────────

character-
measure of
our life.

upon his
deathbed
he requested
a woman.

---

life-
prison of
our making.

---

life-idiot's joke.

Richard L. Narver

my wife
(thank God)
said she
was enjoying
her life.

———————

after life-
what do
the dead
say?

———————

though dying
he couldn't
stop laughing.

———————

"our problem"
(not death)-
an absurd
life.

the king-
never knew
he was
naked as
he stood
before his
people-
promising
them a
better life.

───────────

reality
(despite illusion)
simply is-
and regrettably
only is.

Richard L. Narver

the solipsist-
(forever)
looking for
light.

---

we can
have vision
but not
be able
to see
what is.

---

people change
(even friends)
everything changes.

existential abyss - home sweet home.

Richard L. Narver

policy
(generally)
written by
self-serving
idiots.

---

hmo
plague
economic virus.

---

policy
(generally)
crafted to
prohibit what
is needed.

evil
hard for us
to see…
if you
don't see it
it will
kill you.

---

if
someone hurts
you once,
they will
hurt you twice.

Richard L. Narver

i hesitate
on the path-
to nothingness.

---

nothingness-
(unfortunately)
omnipresent.

---

eternal life
(most likely)
an illusion
caused by
fear of
nothingness.

---

think
(clearly)
about your
life and death.

life-
wasted on
chasing illusion.

---

see
(without illusion)
your life.

---

life's shadows
slowly fade
away.

---

dear God,
what is
our purpose?

Richard L. Narver

life- sometimes too long.

sad songs
(unfortunately)-
play forever.

---

meaning
(most likely)
our invention.

---

rarely-
do we
see.

---

truth-
rarely seen
but in
our heart.

Richard L. Narver

good-by-
always comes.

———————————

the past
is dead-
let it
rest in
peace.

———————————

we seek
(unfortunately)-
light
in
darkness.

the subtle
(clearly seen)-
exposes truth.

---

truth-
present but
rarely seen.

---

the light
is present-
see it.

---

good fortune
fool's dream.

---

my friend-
truth is
your companion
forever.

Richard L. Narver

belief-
blind helmsman
in high seas.

wagon wheel hangs from ceiling-
light and shadow dance between spokes
rolls on rolls on
dusty
past gnarled roots and forgotten bones-
team heads for red rock
rolls on rolls on
bringing voices back.

Richard L. Narver

sunset-
soft sound
from field or wood
lingers in
the air.

---

after
toil of
day
sun rests on pine ridge
its energy spent.

the rain
fell upon
the graveyard
and made
it easier
to dig
new graves.

———————

as the
coffin began
to close
the corpse
(oddly)
seemed to
be smiling.

———————

death of young people leaves a permanent scar
on the heart.

Richard L. Narver

failure- lesson for success.

i
have seen
more than
i wanted
to see.

---

don't try
to walk
on water-
it can't
be done.

---

think
about tomorrow-
it comes
too soon.

Richard L. Narver

x
its meaning needed
to see in darkness.

---

truth-
our invention
nothing more.

---

we
(unfortunately)
search for
meaning that
has never
existed.

---

belief
(though blind)
sees light.

nothingness
(most likely)
our destiny.

---

transient ciphers
(fearing death)
waste their
moment
in illusion.

---

reality
(despite illusion)
simply is-
and regrettably
only is.

---

see
(clearly)
what is
in the eyes.

Richard L. Narver

despair's
cold breeze
blows out
the candle.

---

our life-
hilarious in sorrow.

---

the dead
(without exception)
are dead-
forever.

---

our life
(generally)
wasted time.

life
(unfortunately)
is what
it is

───────────

suddenly (without warning)-
lost moment.

───────────

our eyes
(truly seen)
tell our story.

───────────

anxiety-
reaction to
our existential
predicament.

───────────

hope-
life's joke.

Richard L. Narver

life
(only)
is.

———————

dreams
far away-
but not
impossible
to reach.

———————

we
(too often)
have seen
what we
never wanted
to see.

we
(blindly)
seek truth
that has
never existed.

---

see truth-as it is.

---

pain
too intense-
screams for
God's mercy.

---

the shepherd
protecting
his flock-
was eaten
by wolves.

Richard L. Narver

life
(as is)
rarely seen.

―――――――――

truth
(present)
see it.

―――――――――

time
(without hesitation)-
travels too fast.

―――――――――

sequence
is inherent
in reality-
and time
is our
invention to
measure it.

it is
the little
things in
life that
i haven't
been able
to figure
out.

---

see patterns
of behavior
they will
be there.

---

joy
(please)
nurture it.

Richard L. Narver

our death
like the
next day-
always comes.

---

our life
(generally)
a joke.

---

meaning
(most likely)
a delusion.

---

purpose-
Phideppide's run.

---

see people
(though painful)
as they are.

the sea
spray
hits
the bow
of the
boat and
flavors
my scotch.

───────────────

flower smiles
into new
day.

Richard L. Narver

a cougar
screams
with the
rising of
the sun.

---

suns rays
fall between
the redwoods-
dew drops
glisten on
the ferns.

---

early evening
symphony-
crickets and
frogs in harmony.

a child
came upon
an old peasant
crying next
to a grave.
the child
said,
"why are
you crying?"
the peasant said,
"my wife
has gone
to heaven."
the child said,
"don't cry,
heaven is
a good place."

Richard L. Narver

the homeless
come from
all walks
of life,
and vary
amongst themselves
like all people.

---

however,
there is
one condition
they have
in common -
hunger.

prejudice
of any
kind
destroys the
heart.

---

harm
the homeless
and you
will lose
your soul.

Richard L. Narver

a beggar
wandering in
the wilderness
came upon
a treasure chest
full of
gold and silver.
the beggar
dug a deep hole
and buried
the treasure chest.
thereafter
the beggar
spent the rest
of his days
worrying about
losing his
great wealth-
until he died of starvation.

prejudice
comes in
all shapes,
sizes and
colors.
for the
more discriminating
there is
age, sex,
religion and status.
for the more
imaginative
there is
psychiatric diagnosis
dietary preference
and astrological signs.
there is
no end to it.
something for
everyone.
prejudice-
here to stay.

Richard L. Narver

philosophy
is the
study
of what
we will
never know
but will
always
want to
know.

———————

learn from
the past
but don't
carry it
with you.

chicks find
sleeping worms
in the grass
a hawk
circles overhead.

───────────

waves crest
under moon
crabs crawl
over kelp
herring run
with tide.

───────────

waves crash
against the
cliff-
young gull
soars overhead.

Richard L. Narver

our destination
(most likely)
is nothingness
but enjoy
the journey.

———————

they lived
and died
in darkness
never knowing
their darkness
was self-
imposed.

———————

people
without vision
(poor souls)
see races
rather than
human beings.

our greatest
challenge
(my friend)
is eliminating
cruelty.

Richard L. Narver

the cougar's
steps were
not heard-
as it
stalked
the hunter.

---

pre dawn-
the mist
lies briefly
upon the
fields so
fresh and
sweet.

Fall's light
(like life)
quickly turns
to darkness.

Agates in the Sand

on the summit
among resonant
voices of pine-
Plato becomes
clear.

---

poetry-
(best words)
come from
bread and
wine.

Richard L. Narver

to be simple - isn't easy.

dear b.j.
i wish
time would
go away
and leave
us alone.

Richard L. Narver

(Clint and Nikki)
you are
the prize
of my
life, and
my heart
will always
be with you.
believe
in yourself
and fulfill
your dreams.

my dream
(ultimately) -
shaking hands
with God.

Richard L. Narver

Final words:

despite what
i have
written about
reality -
there may
be something
beyond it -

_____

my friends-
(be kind)
i love
you and
wish you
the best

—Dick Narver
1942 - 2009